Why is Collin Like That?

by: dr. Bruce

illustrated by: Amanda Parks

PRESS

Why is Collin Like That?
by dr. Bruce

Printed in the United States of America

ISBN 9781609579791

www.xulonpress.com

This book is dedicated to
all children with a brother or sister
with a disability.

I HEAR YOU!

– dr. Bruce

About the Illustrator

Amanda is a young, blossoming artist; that I met at a voice-over for a book. She was sitting in the corner, doodling. Her youthful, sensitive and creative spirit was all I needed to illustrate this emotional, feeling story. I am looking forward to collaborating with her talent, as she uniquely polishes a finished word creation into a beautiful living work of art.

– dr. Bruce

A Note from the Illustrator

I'd like to thank Tara so much for giving me this opportunity to draw all these pictures for her and her book! It was quite an experience.
– Amanda

To see Amanda's artwork:
www.destructivepandas.deviantart.com

Everyday my brother Collin,
behaves the same old way,

He kicks, screams, and hollers,
and why he will not say.

He never has an answer,
when I ask him why he screams,

My mother always tells me,
he's not trying to be mean.

"God made Collin special,"
is my mothers one reply.

I really don't understand,
and no-one will tell me why.

He breaks my toys and rips my things, and won't do what I ask,

My mother says for Collin,
it is too difficult a task.

Finally I asked my mom,
"Why is Collin such a pain?"

"It is hard," my mother replied, "but I will try to explain."

God made Collin special,
the term is called PDD,

He can not help the way he feels;
he is different than you and me.

It is hard for him to learn,
the easy things you do,

So sometimes he gets angry, but it's not because of you.

So next time Collin is upset,
and appears to misbehave,

Show patience for his actions,
and forgive as God forgave.

I love my little brother;
I guess he's not so bad,

For God has given him to me,
for this I am so glad.

This page was created just for you!

How does it make you feel when your brother or sister becomes angry, frustrated, or breaks your things for reasons you don't understand?

Use this page to show how this makes you feel!

Drawings, scribbles, faces…it's your special page!

Have you finished your page?
Great!
When you are ready, it is important to talk to someone about what you have drawn.

Did you talk with someone?

How do you feel now?

Use this page to show how you are feeling after you were able to share your page with someone and talk about your feelings.

Never forget that Jesus is your friend and is available for you to share your feelings with all of the time!
He never sleeps…He is never too busy…He only cares about and loves YOU!

Discussion Page

1. How would you define a negative feeling?

2. Do you know that it is O.K. to have feelings that are negative about someone else?

3. What are the best ways for you to share your thoughts?

4. Who are you able to trust with those feelings?

5. Do you feel responsible for your situation?

6. It is O.K. to take care of you. Here are some positive ways:

    A. Go on a special event with a friend or parent.
    B. Remove yourself to do a project that you enjoy.
    C. Tell an adult that it is time for you. Tell an adult that you need "alone time".
    D. Ride your bike; go for a walk. Physical activity is best.

LaVergne, TN USA
02 January 2010
210730LV00005B